Ayr Ontario in Photos, Saving Our History One Photo at a Time

Photography
by Barbara Raué
2012

Series Name:
Cruising Ontario

Book 21: Ayr

Cover photo: Swans and ducks on Cedar Creek by Jedburgh Dam which provided water power for the local industries

Series Name: Cruising Ontario

Other Books by Barbara Raue

Coins of Gold

Arrows, Indians and Love

The Life and Times of Barbara
Volume 1: Inventions That Have Enhanced My Life
Volume 2: Entertainment That I Have Enjoyed
Volume 3: East Coast Trips
Volume 4: Olympics
Volume 5: Wonders of the World
Volume 6: Caribbean Cruises
Volume 7: Animals
Volume 8: Storms

Ayr

Ayr is located south of Kitchener and west of Cambridge, and south of Highway 401.

In 1824, Abel Mudge built a saw mill and flour mill at the junction of Cedar Creek and the Nith River. This was the first of three settlements, Jedburgh in the east (Main Street), Nithvale in the west (Piper Street) and Mudge's Mill in the centre (Stanley/Northumberland Streets) in what is today the Village of Ayr.

Jedburgh began in 1832 when John Hall, a young immigrant from Jedburgh, Scotland, purchased a 75-acre parcel of land that included the area now flooded by Jedburgh Dam. By 1850 Hall had developed several industries, including a flour mill, sawmill and distillery with water power provided by the damming of Cedar Creek. At the same time a smaller settlement, Nithvale, was founded to the west of Mudge's Mill where a small sawmill opened along the Nith River.

In 1840 when Robert Wyllie established a post office it was given the name "Ayr", a name influenced by the large number of former Ayrshire, Scotland immigrants who were drawn to Canada by promises of inexpensive, fertile land.

In 1846–47 Daniel Manley's mill was built, William Baker's store was established and John Watson's foundry constructed with Watson's Dam its power reservoir. These three key businesses played large roles in Ayr's early success as did the coming of the Credit Valley Railway in 1879. James Somerville began the first Ayr newspaper in 1854.

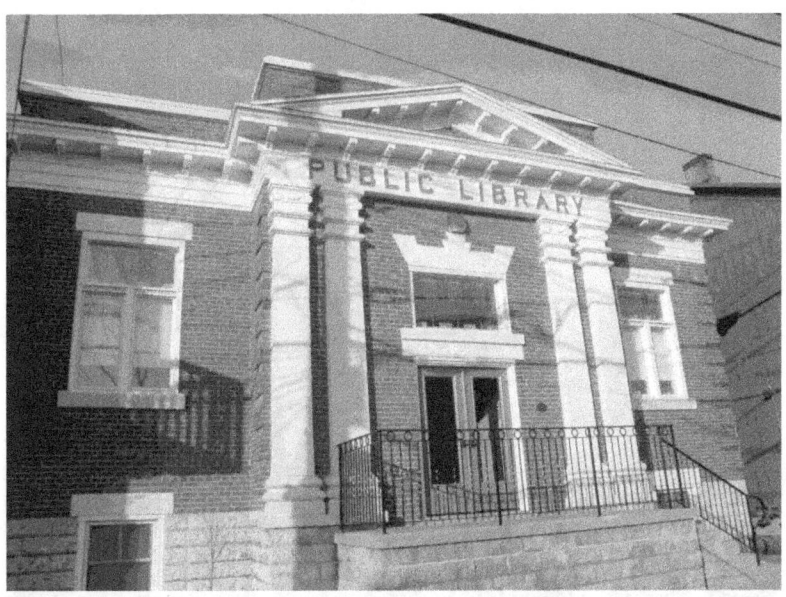

A subscription library was started in Ayr in the 1840s. Andrew Carnegie was asked for a grant to build a library and in 1909 Ayr became the smallest community in Ontario to receive a Carnegie grant. In 1911, the library moved into the building at 92 Stanley Street where it remained for 94 years. In 2004, the library moved into a newer 7,000-square-foot building at 137 Stanley Street, leaving this neoclassical building vacant.

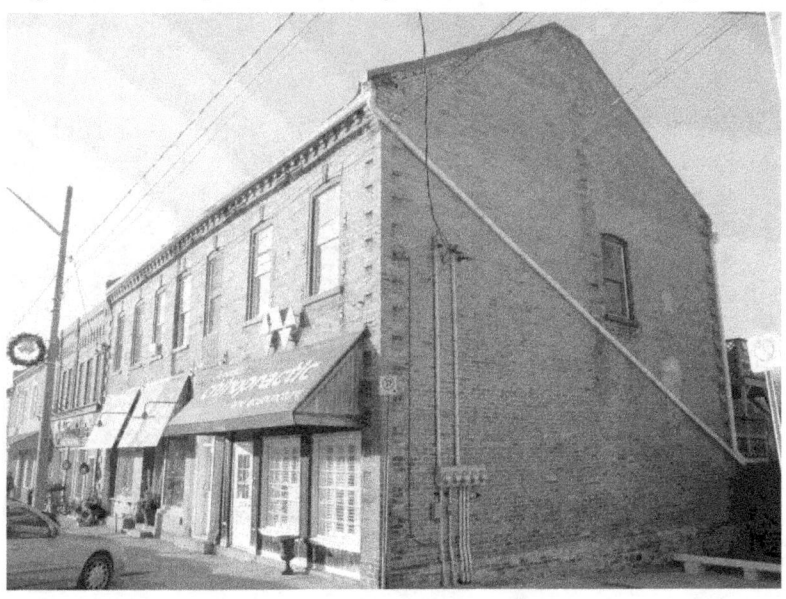

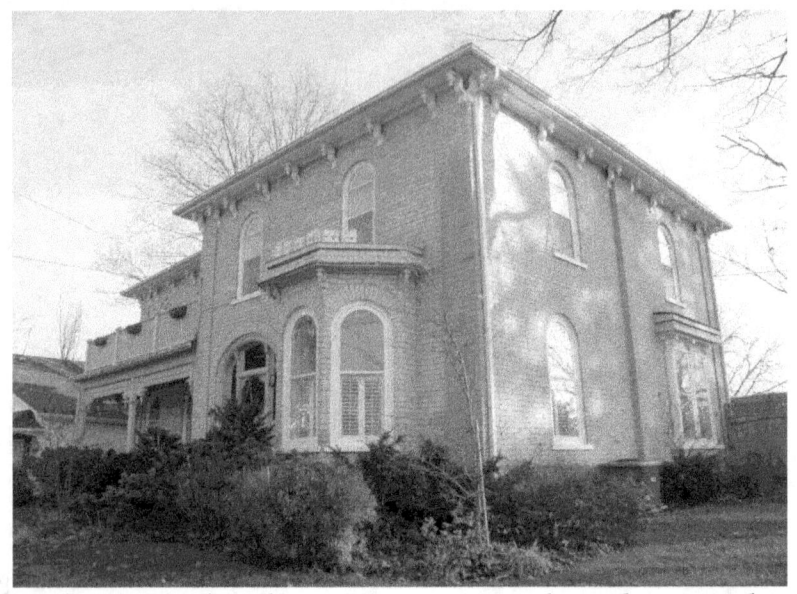

Single cornice brackets, iron cresting above bay window

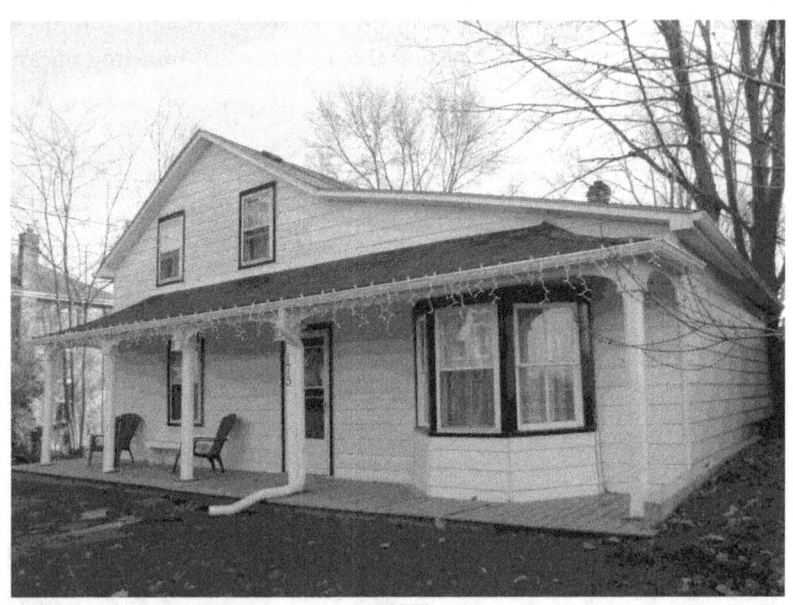

#175

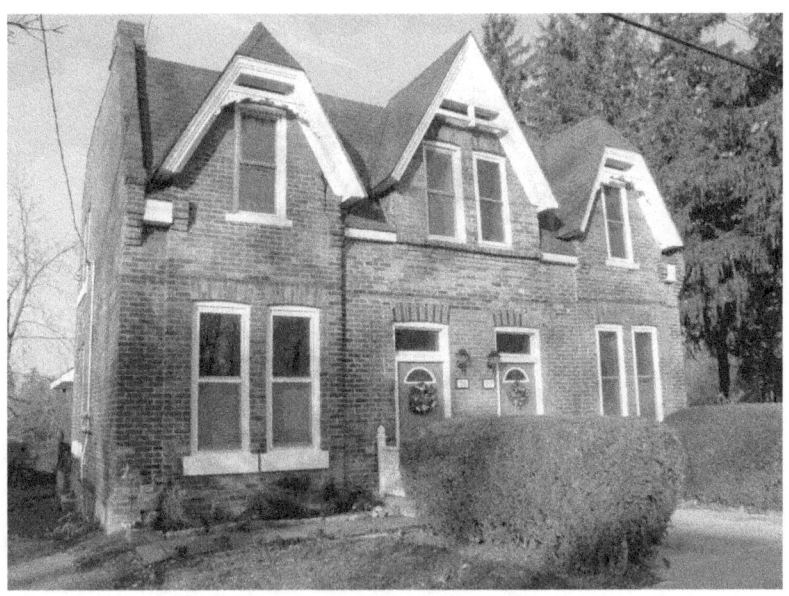

Three Gothic style arches
#190 and #192

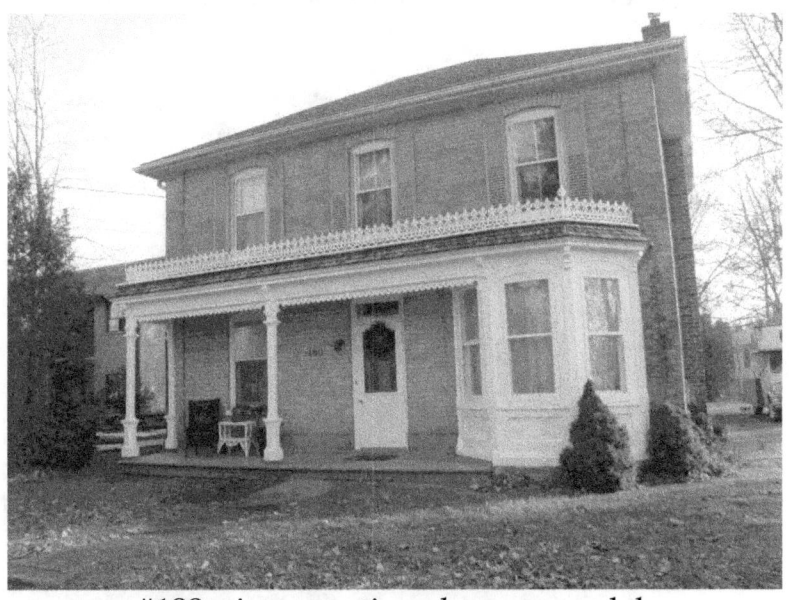

#189 – iron cresting above verandah

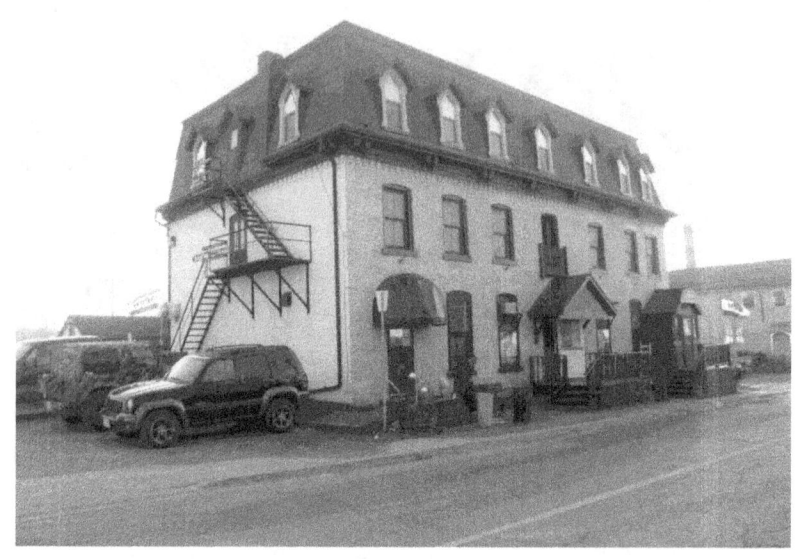

Paired cornice brackets, dentil detailing
Queen's Restaurant and Tavern since 1856

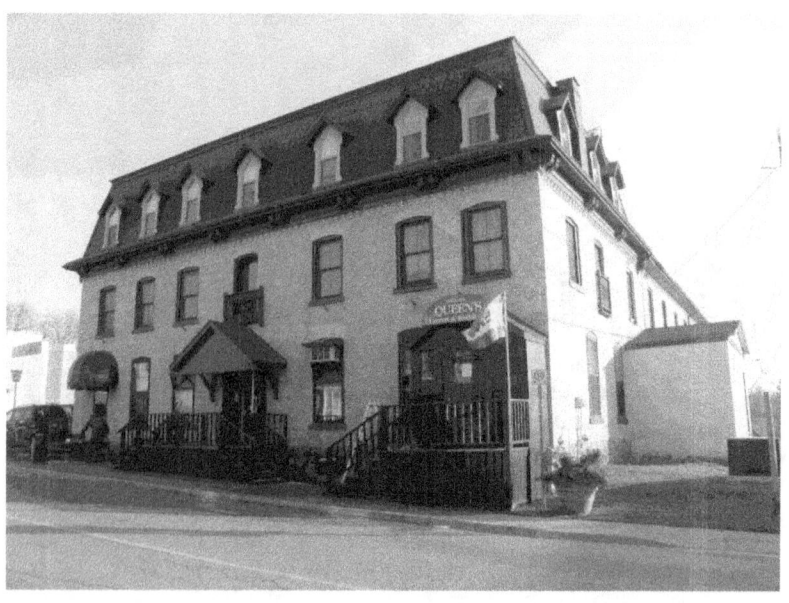

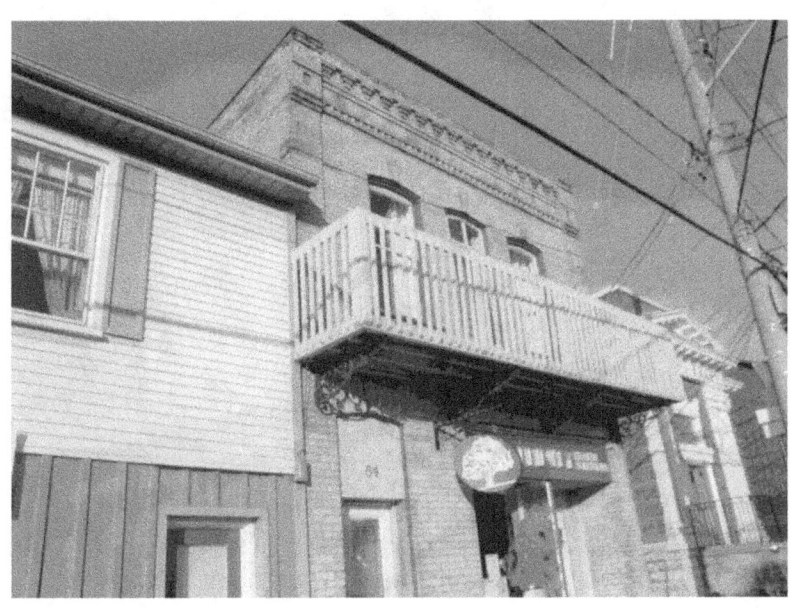

Dichromatic brick detailing

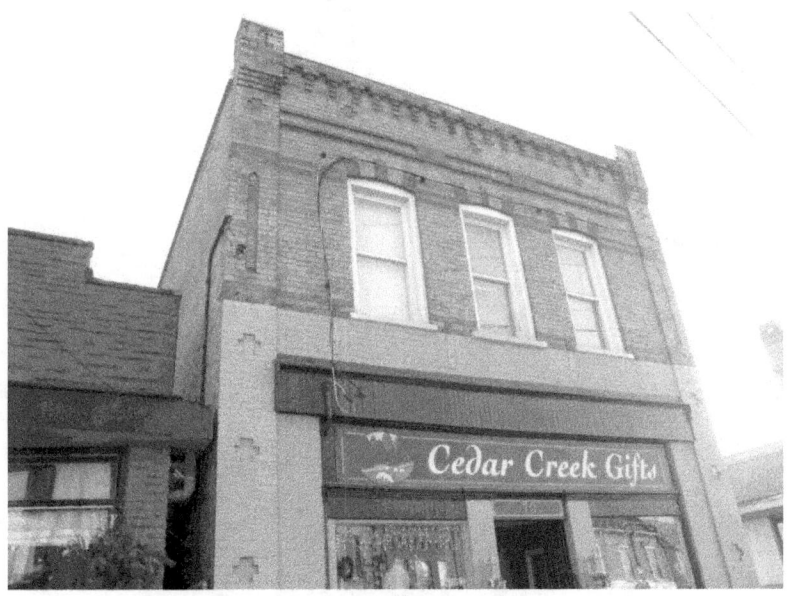

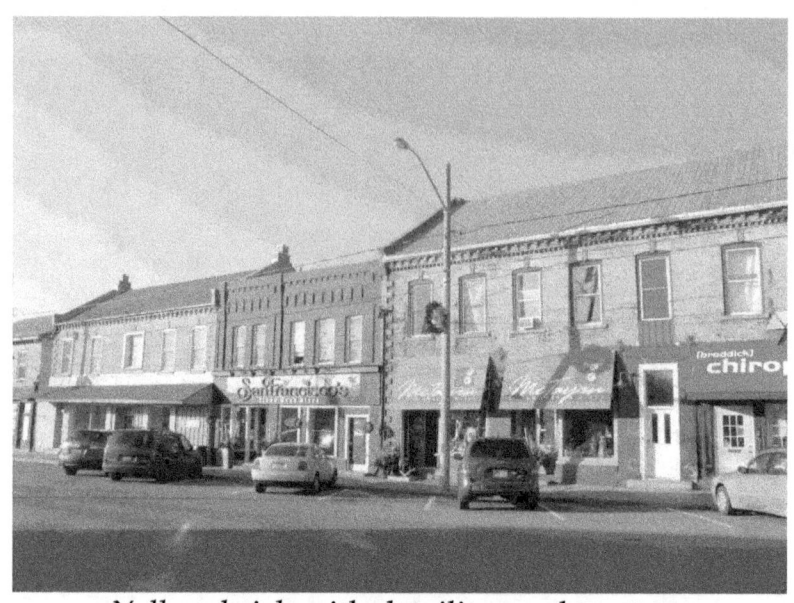

Yellow brick with detailing under eaves

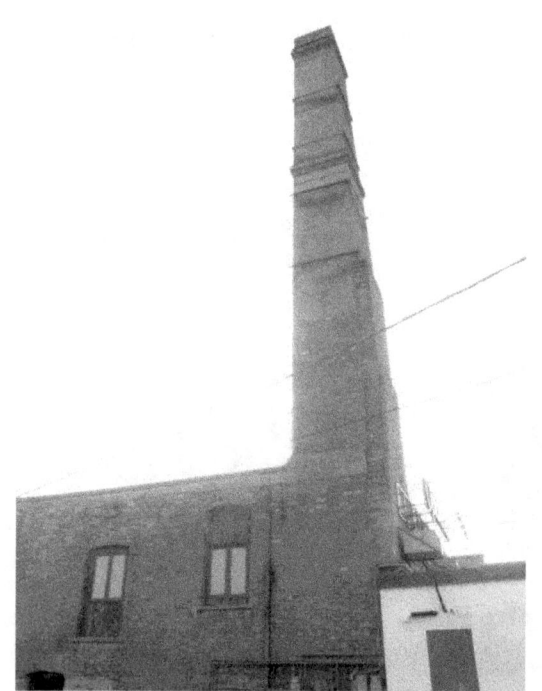

The John Watson Manufacturing Company

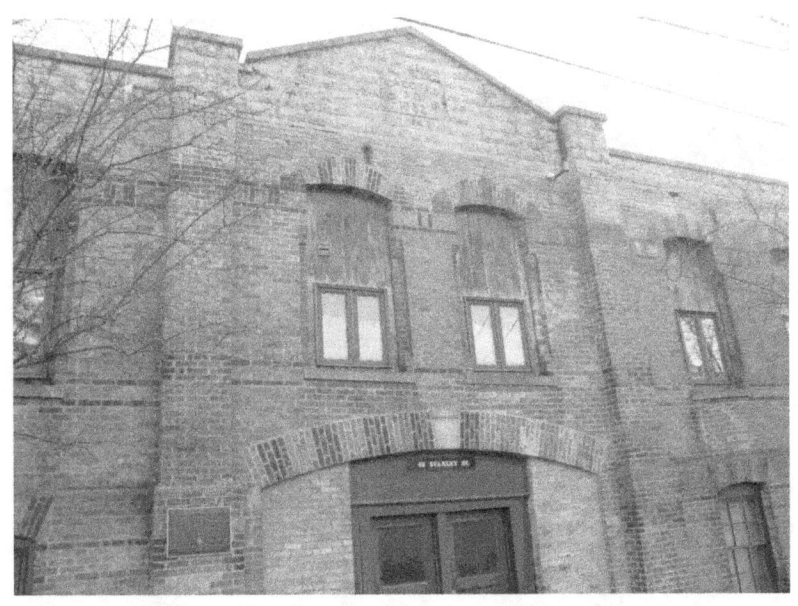

The John Watson Manufacturing Company was founded in 1847 by John Watson, a Scottish moulder and first reeve of Ayr. This building was built in 1882. In continuous family operation for over 127 years, the foundry originally made cast iron pots but expanded into agricultural machinery in the 1880s. It became the largest and best equipped agricultural works in Canada. Over 40 different implements were manufactured with many winning prizes at international exhibitions. Water power was used from 1884 to 1970. In 1920, a fire destroyed the factory and the present two-storey factory was rebuilt from the remains of the original facility.

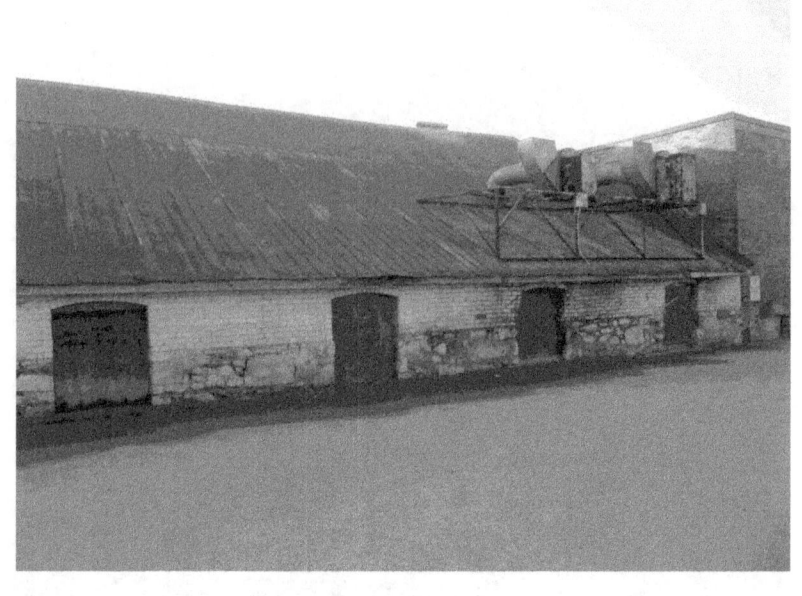

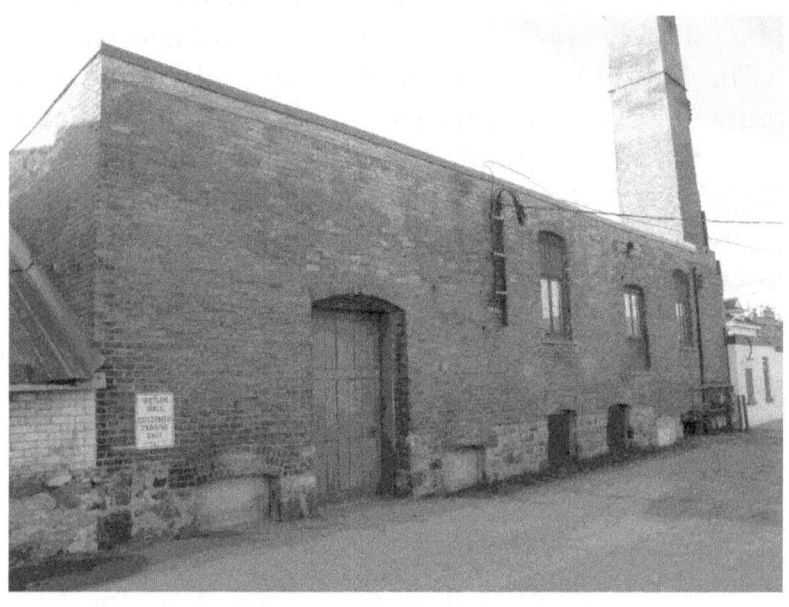

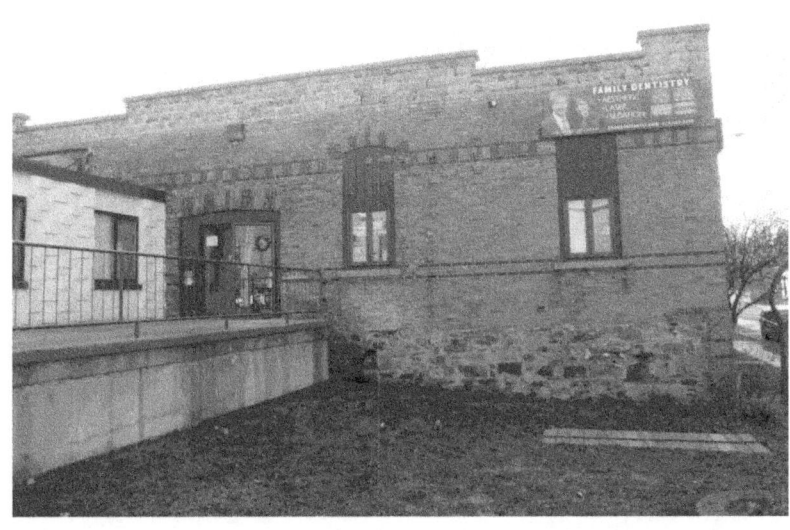

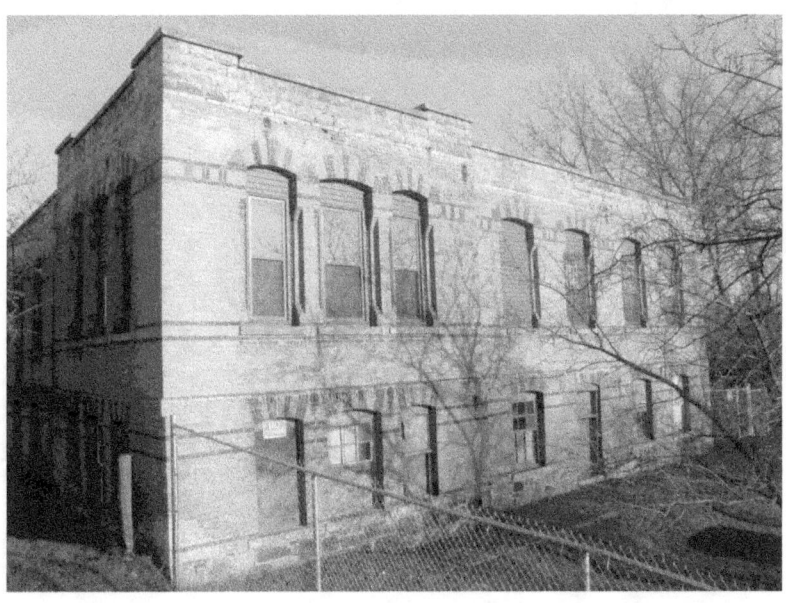

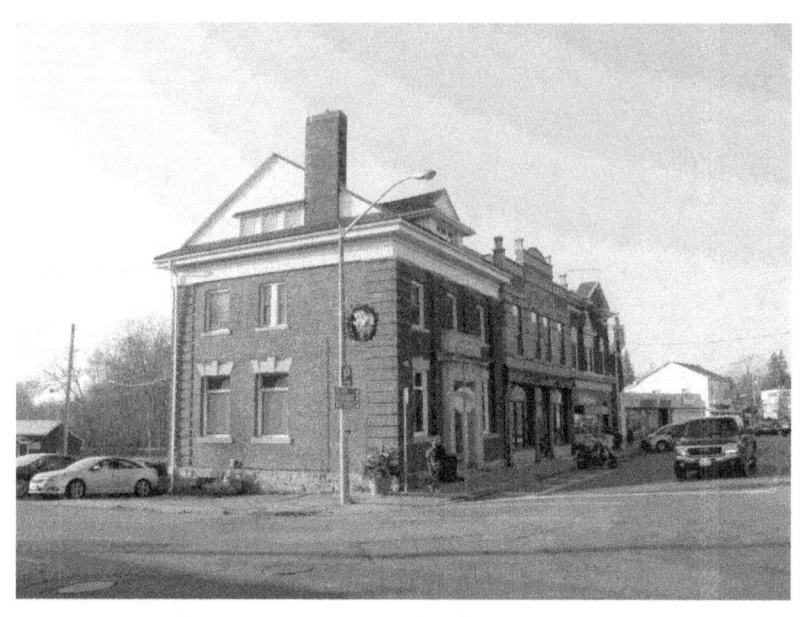

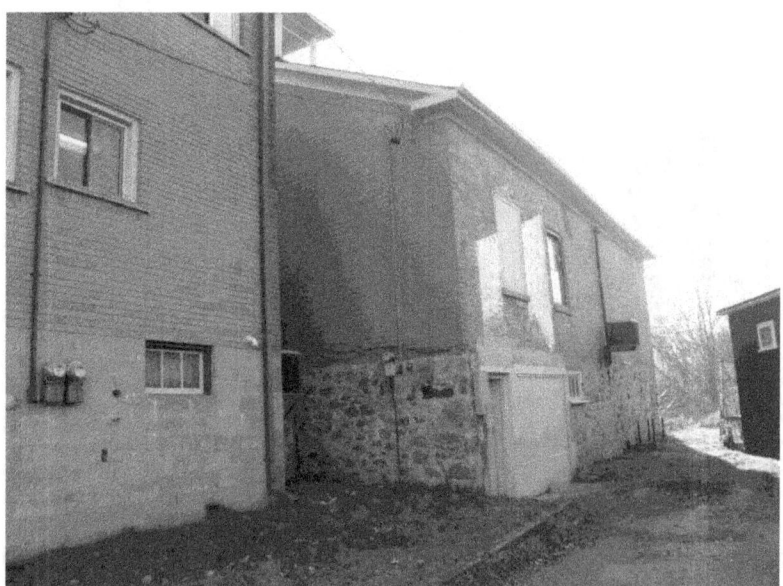

Stone basement

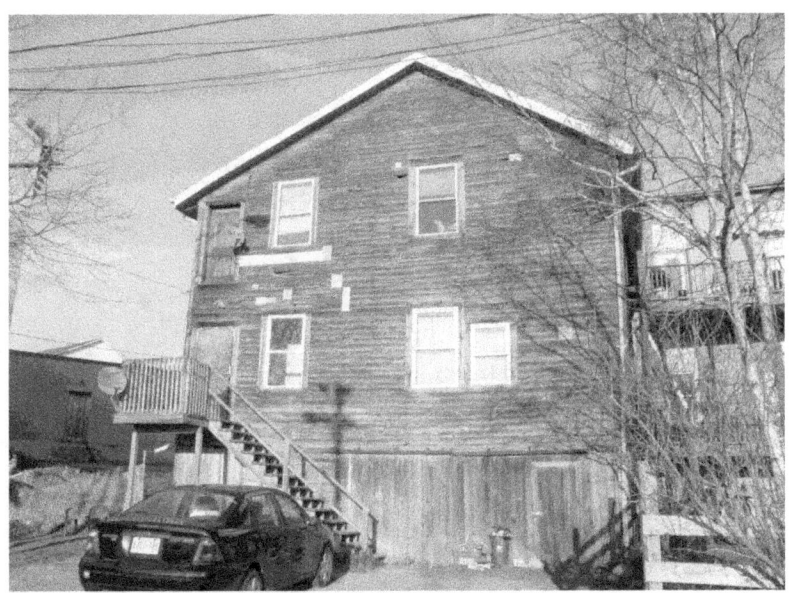

Cedar planking

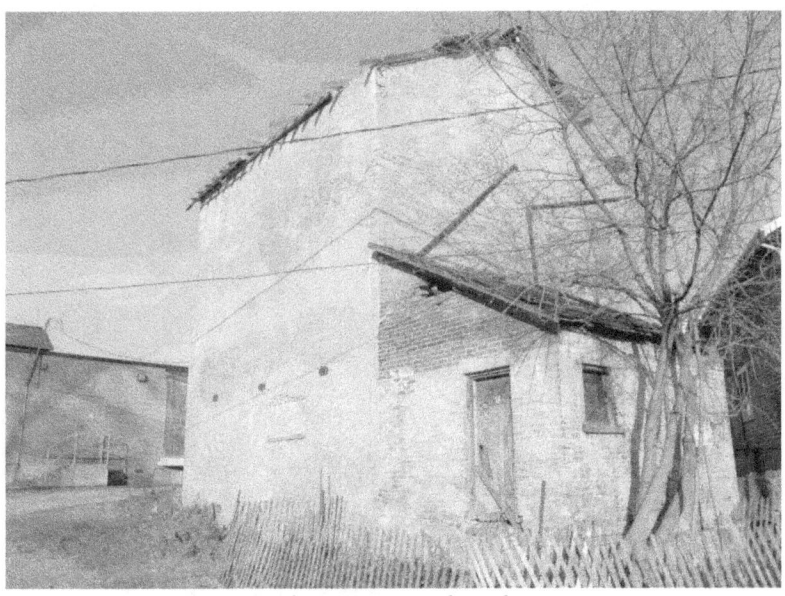

Plaster over brick

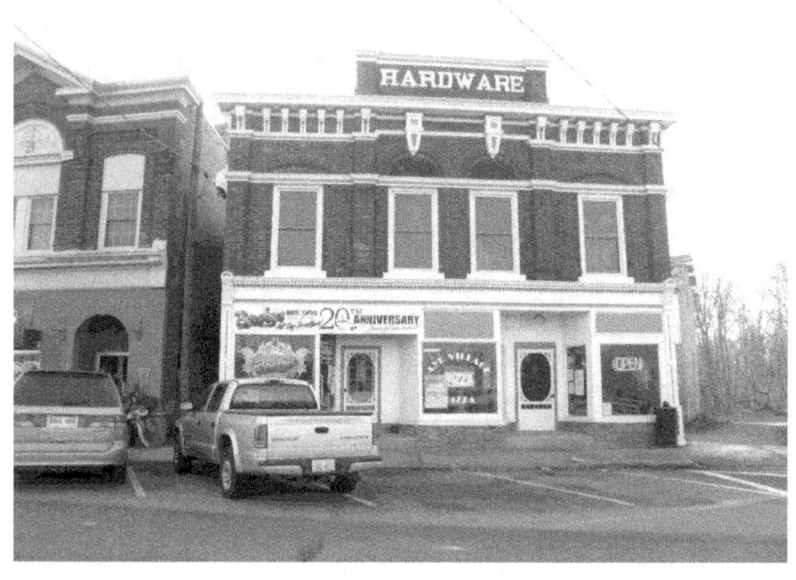

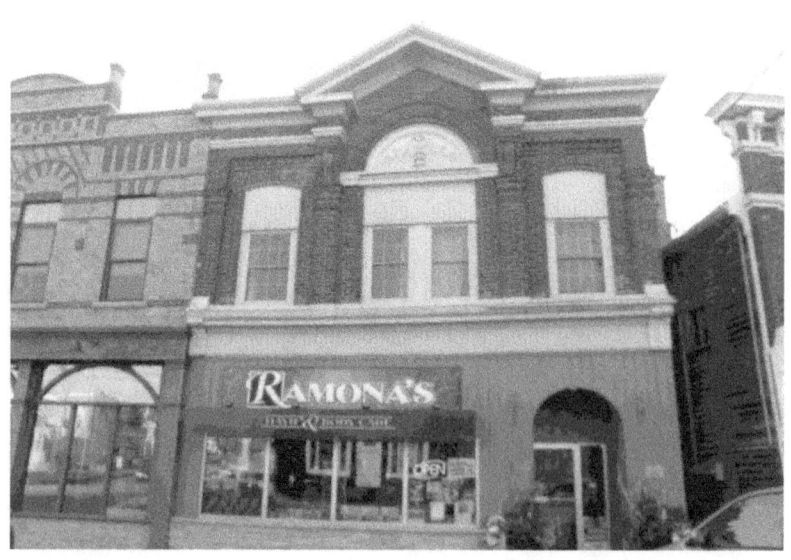

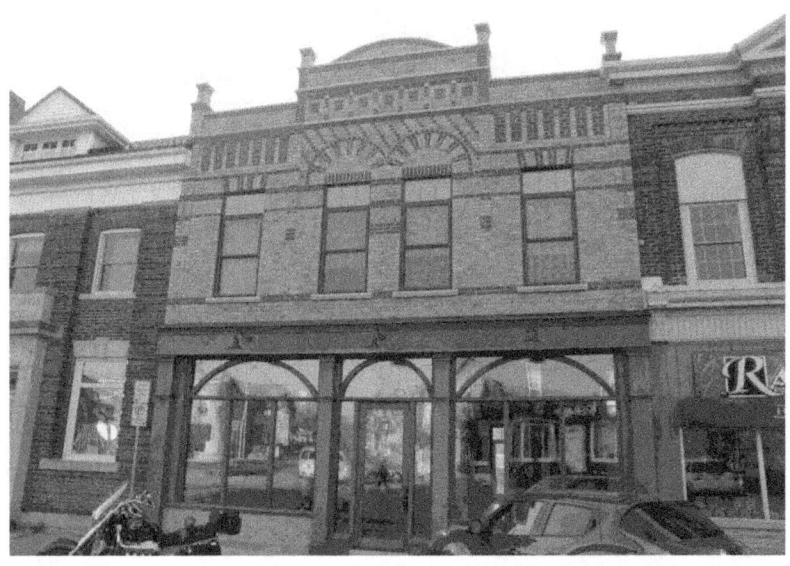

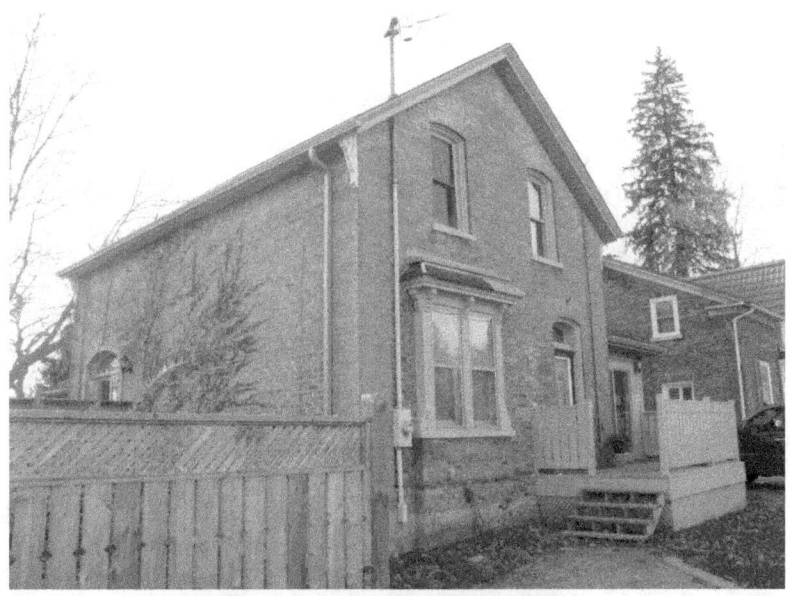

58 Northumberland Street

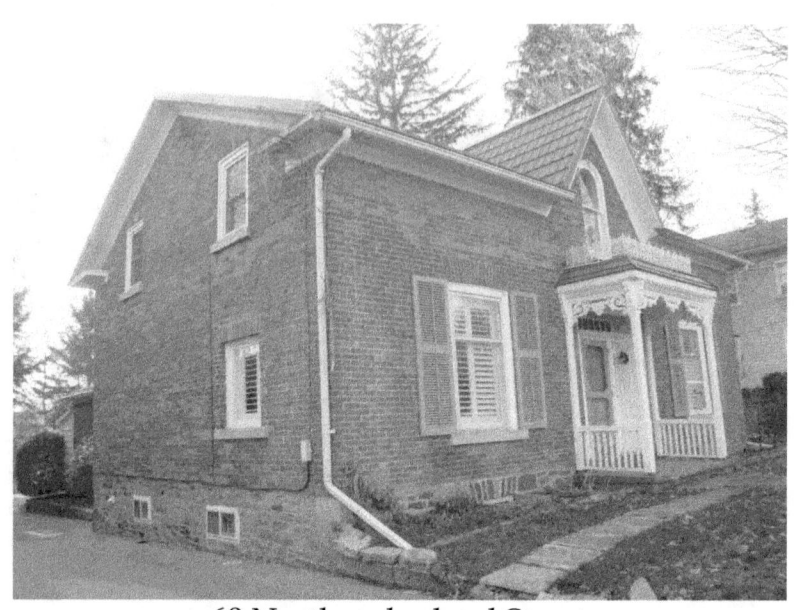

60 Northumberland Street
Iron cresting above the entranceway

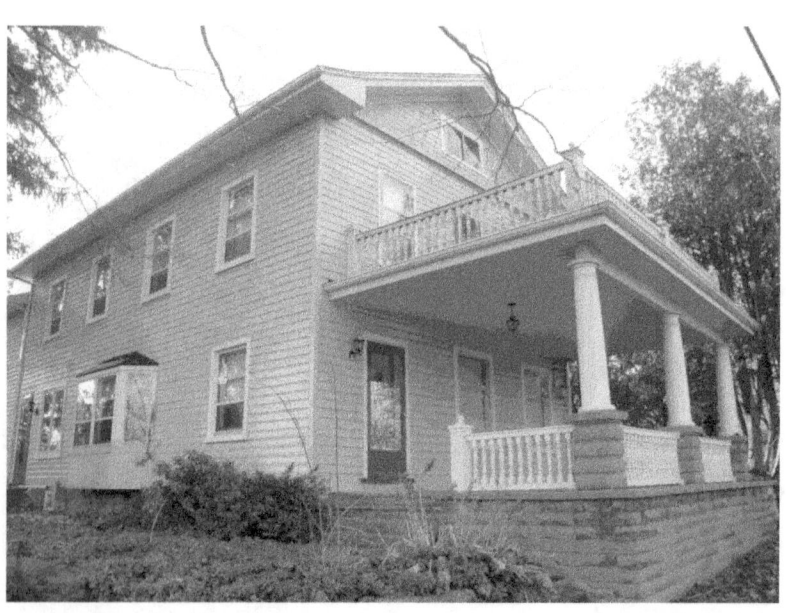

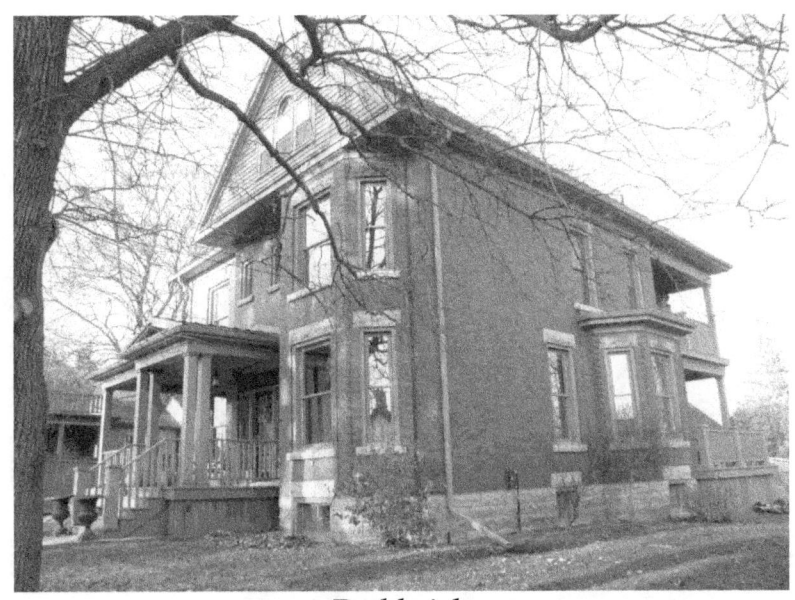

Red brick
81 Northumberland Street

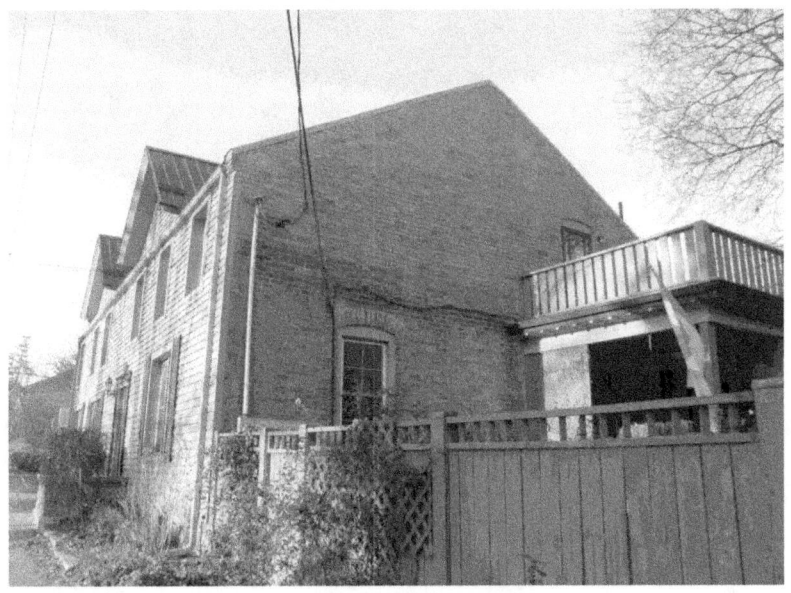

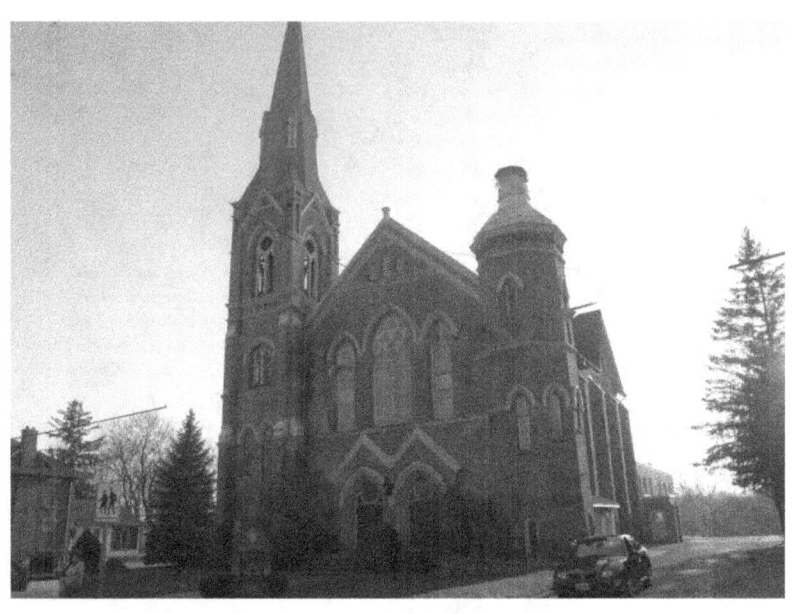

Knox United Church

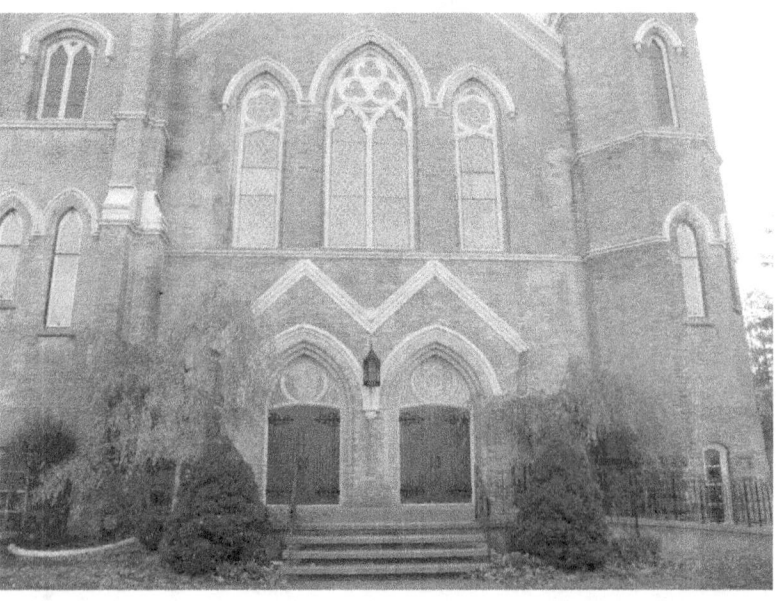

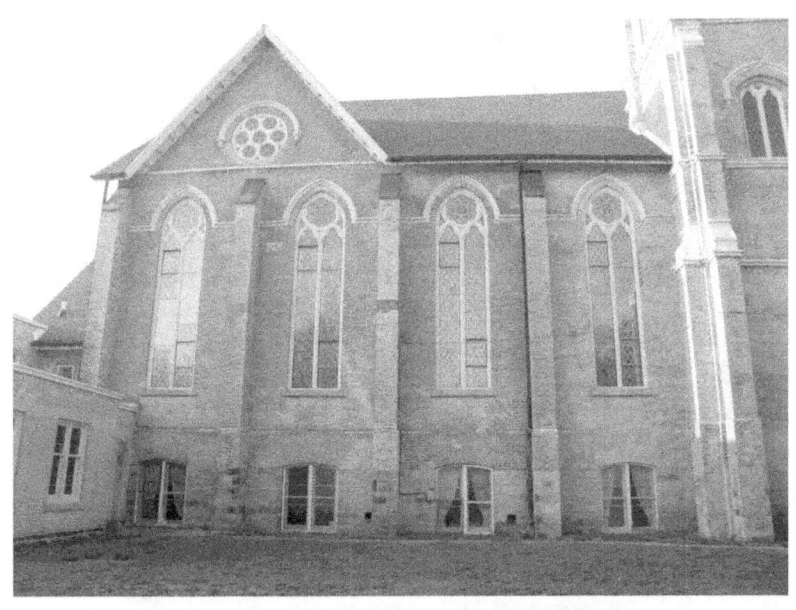

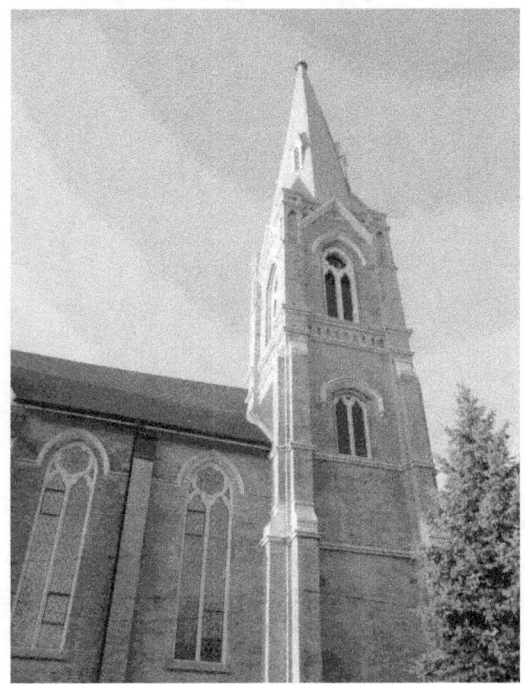

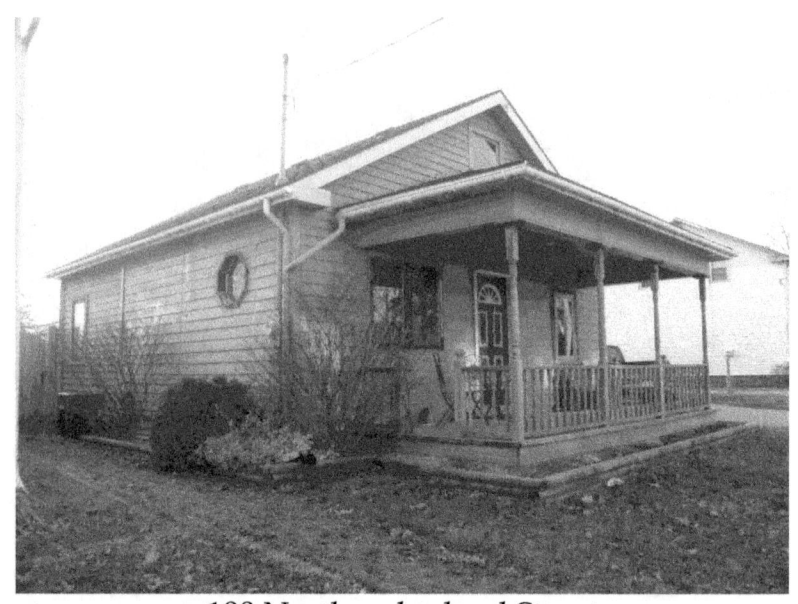

100 Northumberland Street

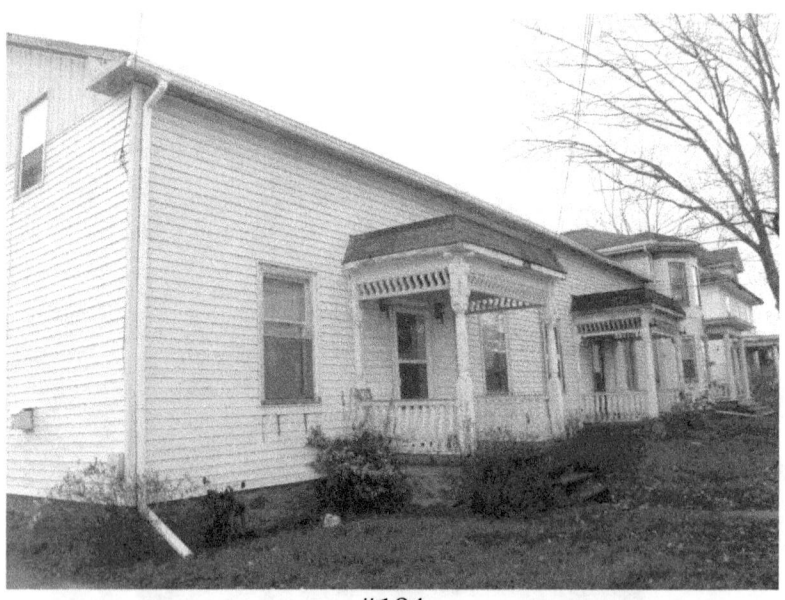

#104

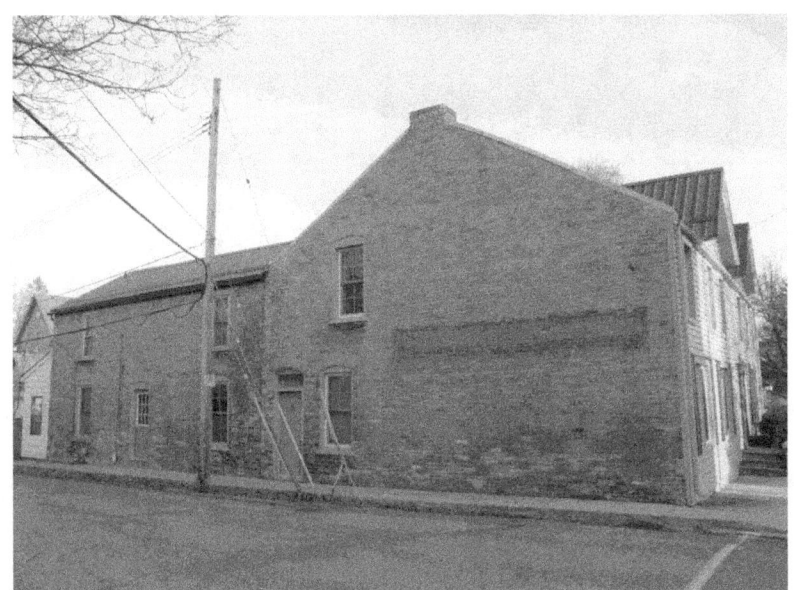

Yellow brick

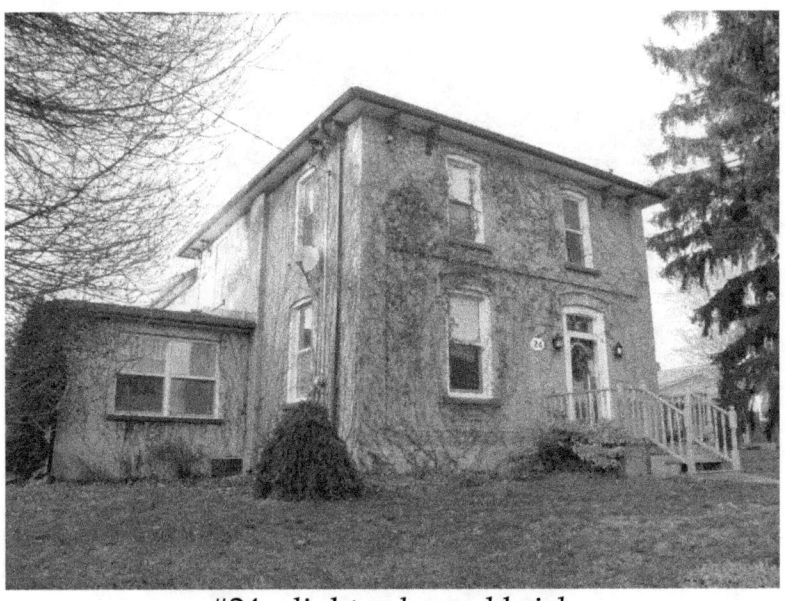

#24 – light coloured brick

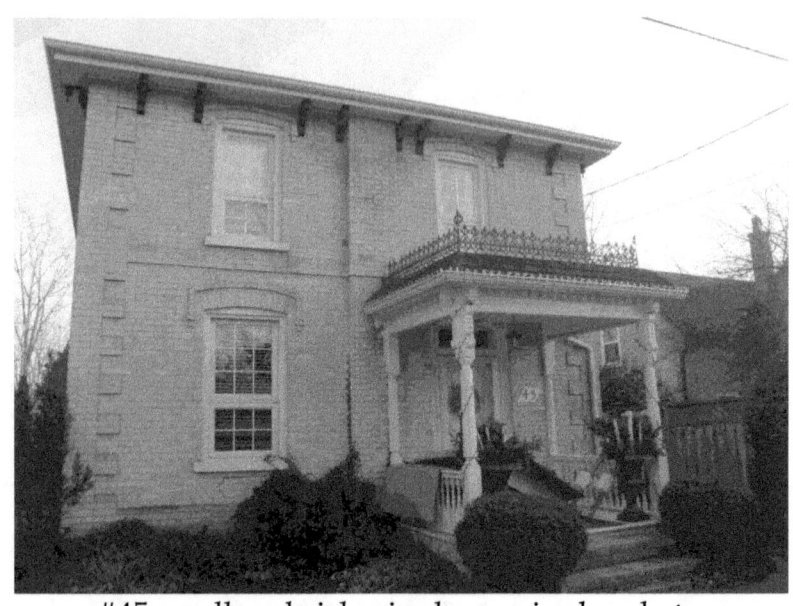

#45 – yellow brick, single cornice brackets,
iron cresting above entranceway

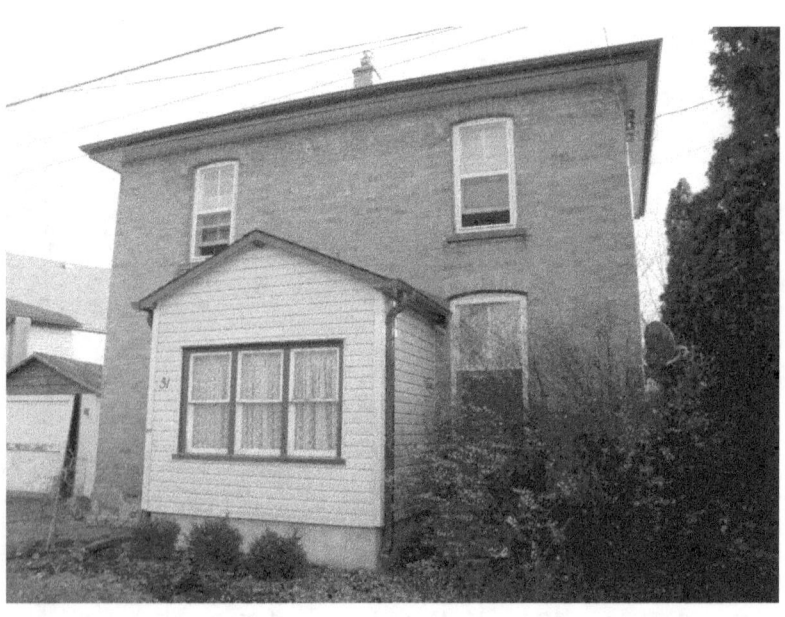

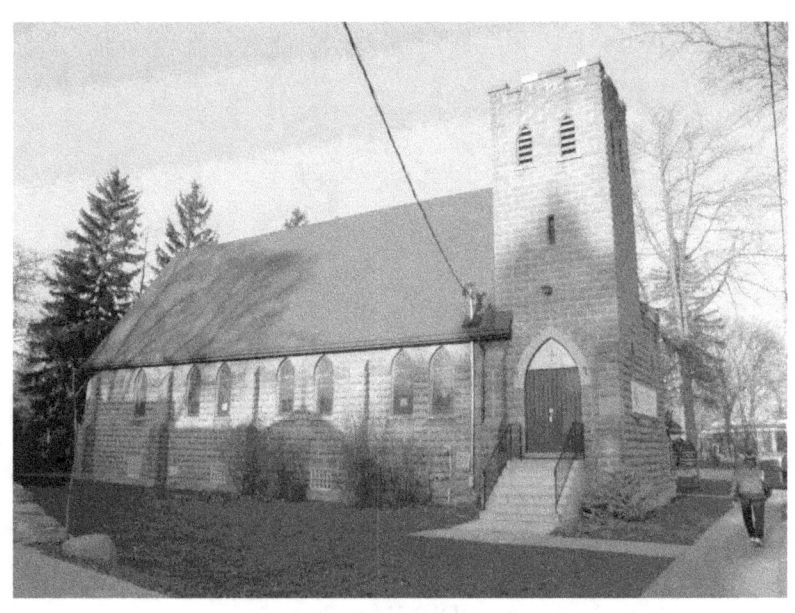

Christian Anglican Church
Celebrating 100 years – 1912-2012

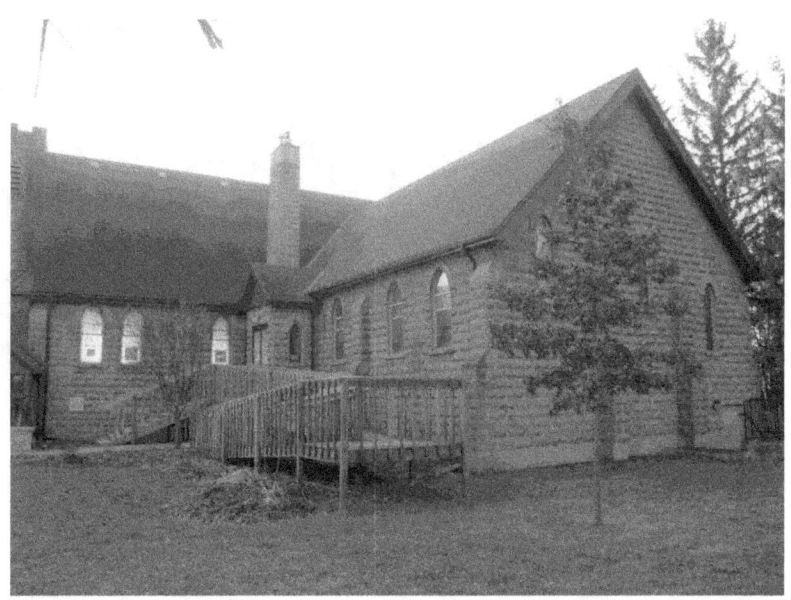

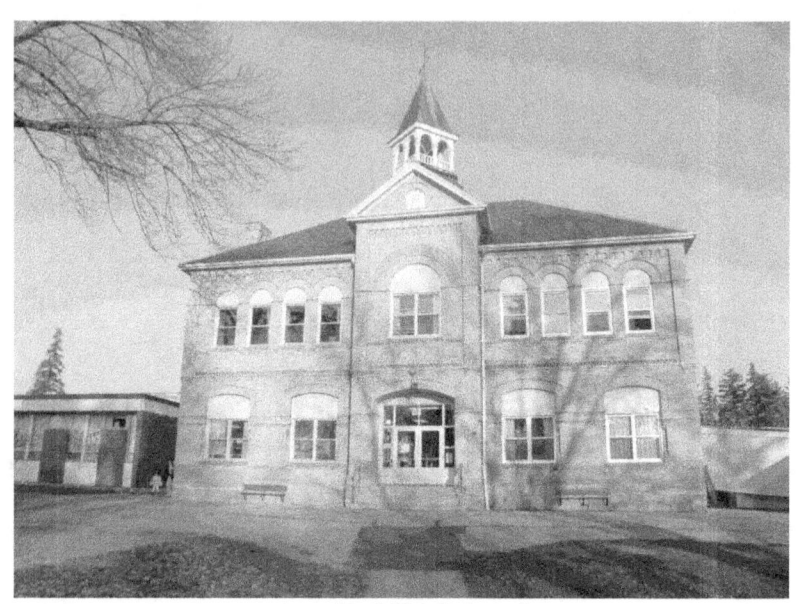

Ayr Public School

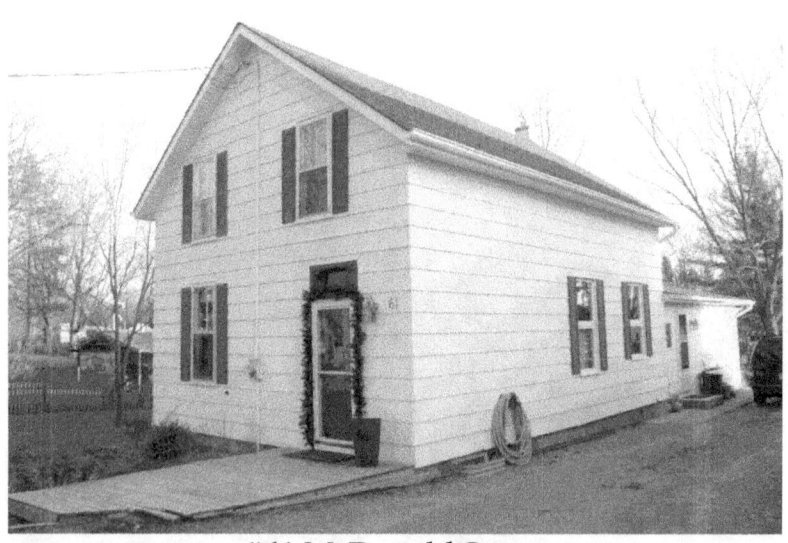

#61 McDonald Street

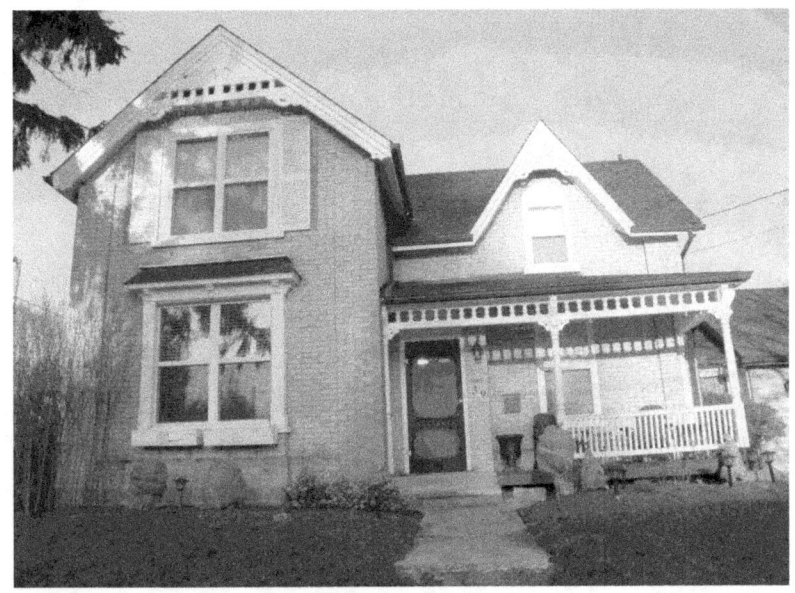

39 McDonald Street

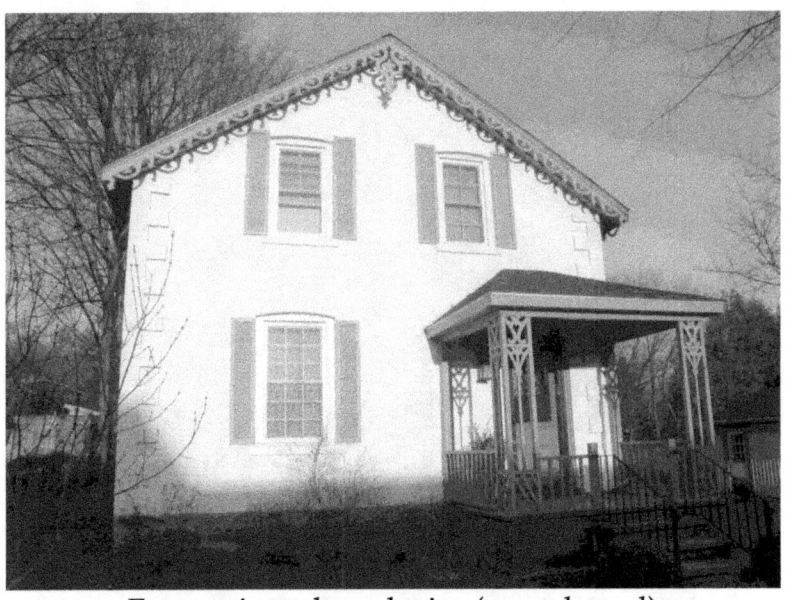

Fancy gingerbread trim (vergeboard)

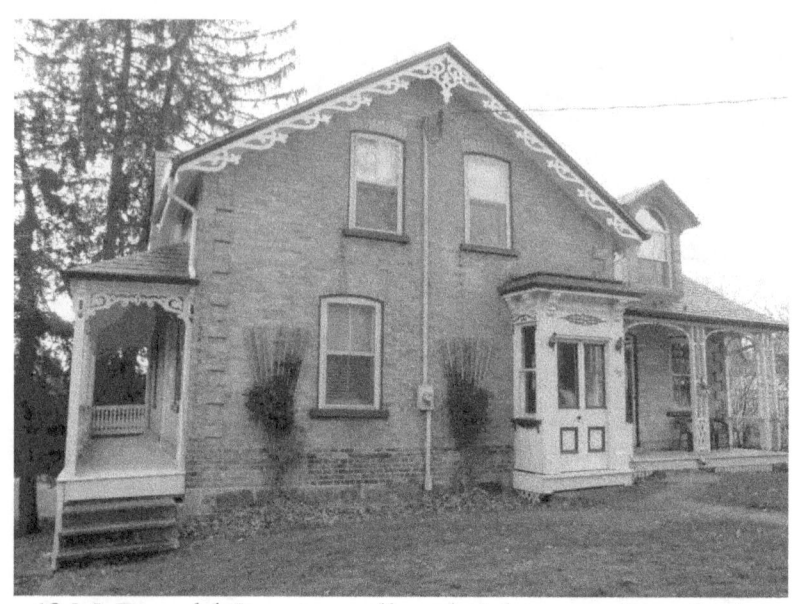

42 McDonald Street – yellow brick, vergeboard trim

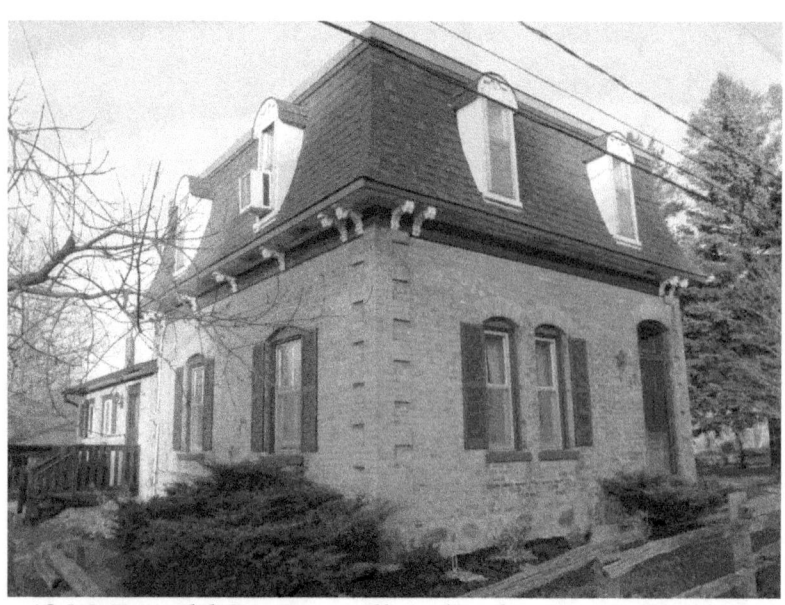

40 McDonald Street – yellow brick, cornice brackets

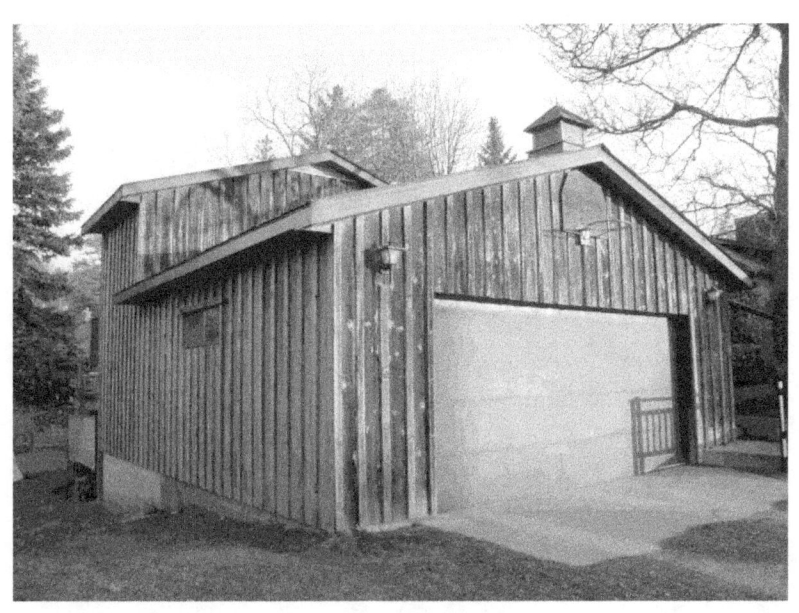

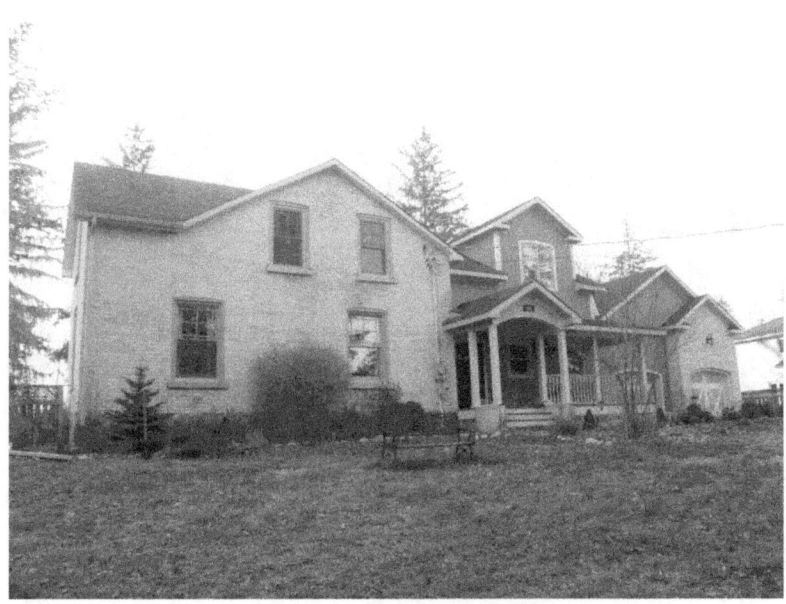

#142 – yellow brick

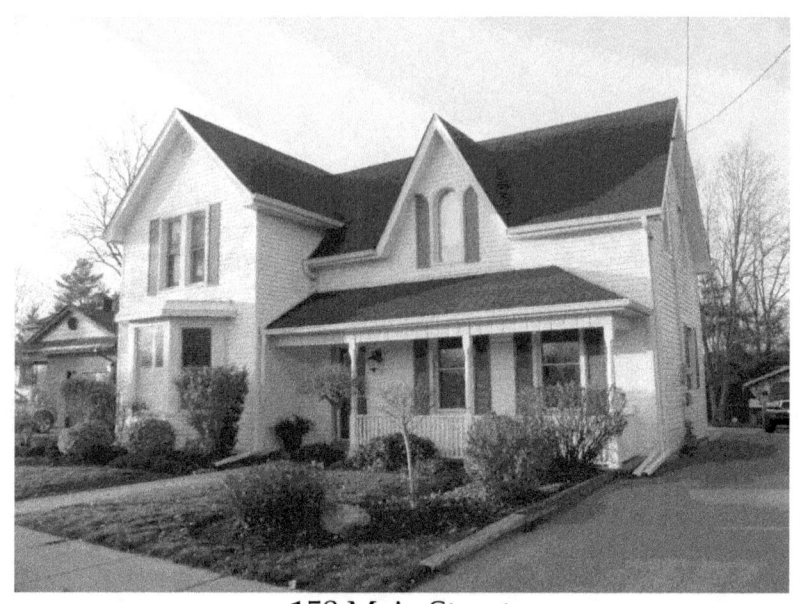

158 Main Street

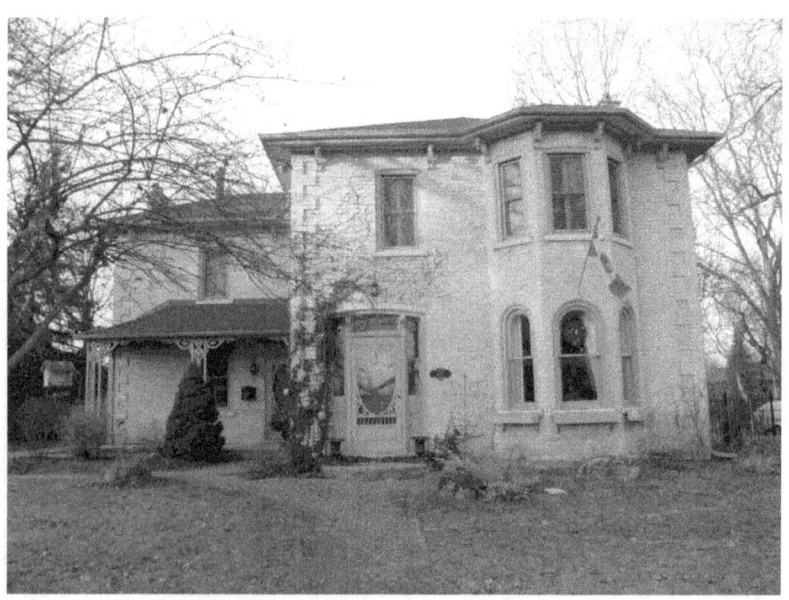

102 Main Street – yellow brick

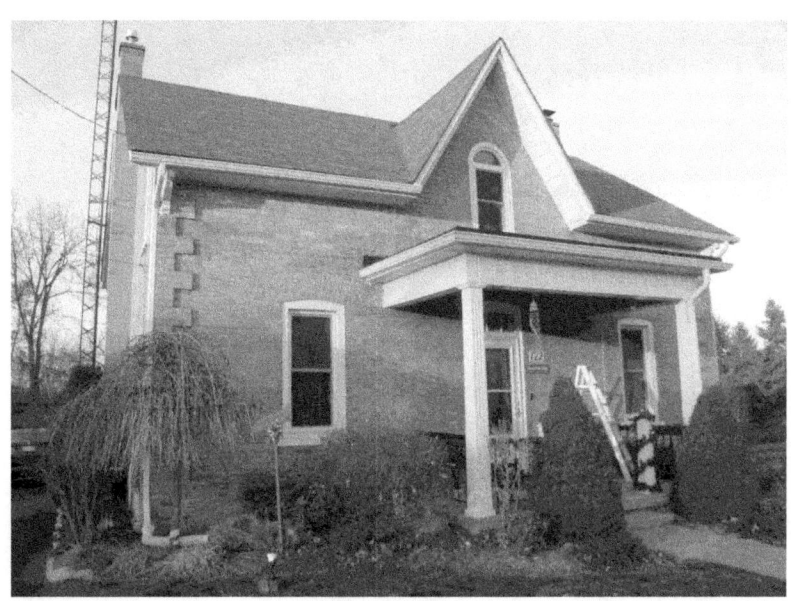

122 Hall Street

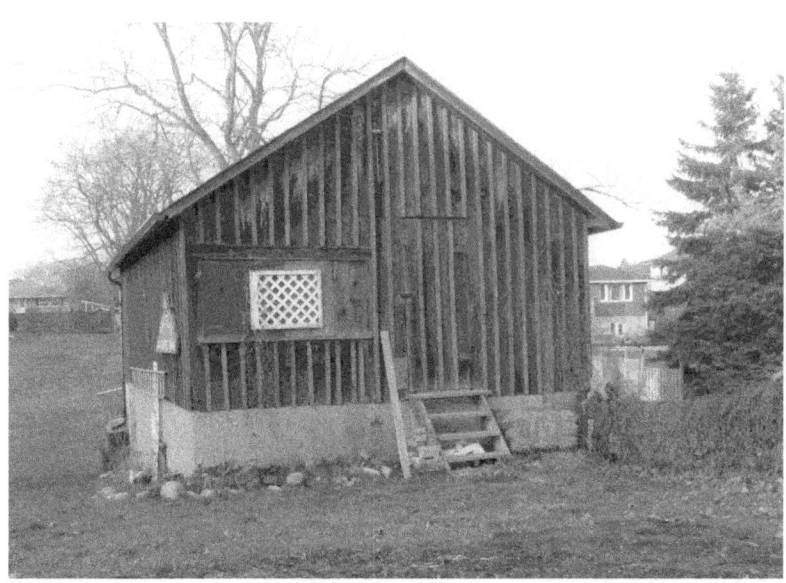

www.ingramcontent.com/pod-product-compliance
Lightning Source LLC
Chambersburg PA
CBHW071600170526
45166CB00004B/1733